RUN
TO WIN

FINDING YOUR LANE
AND FINISHING

Foreword by Bayless Conley
KENNETH MULKEY

PRESS

www.xulonpress.com

DEDICATION

This book is dedicated to my beautiful wife, Angel; my wonderful daughters Ja'nay, Brionna and Destinee; to those who are searching for focus in their spiritual lives as well as those who've been discouraged and stopped following God; to those who are living with eternity in mind, and to those who've not yet entered this race for which Jesus died.

SCRIPTURE

Do you not know that those who run in a race all run, but one receives the prize? Run in such a way that you may obtain it. And everyone who competes for the prize is temperate in all things. Now they do it to obtain a perishable crown, but we for an imperishable crown.

1 Corinthians 9:24-25

ENDORSEMENTS

"Everyone wants their life to matter. Kenneth Mulkey, drawing on a lifetime of experience, has provided insights and application from God's Word that will guide you through the decisions of your life. Run to Win is a book written with you and your future in mind."

– Joel Holm, Pathfinders International

"Truly inspiring, relevant, and motivating! From my perspective as a business owner, this is the perfect, personal book to read multiple times and implement the principles contained therein. The information is easy-to-follow and can be read in one setting. The thought directives at the end of each chapter are challenging, thought-provoking, and designed to take you to the next dimension in your life."

– John Howard, Owner/Operator, Chick-fil-A,
Long Beach, California

"Run To Win shares an essential message where you will discover a clear path to running in your God given greatness. You will see how God's blessings move at the speed of your obedience to Him. This book is for anyone, regardless of what leg of the race you're in, who desires to become a champion for God."

Andrea Anderson Bolder, 2000 Olympic Gold
Medalist, 4 x 400

TABLE OF CONTENTS

FOREWORD

Run To Win is more than a good book. It is more than a collection of clever ideas or motivating thoughts. It is the culmination of decades of faithful service to God and His people. It is a glimpse into the soul of a man that I am blessed to call my friend and co-laborer in ministry.

Kenneth Mulkey has one of the greatest and most balanced preaching/teaching gifts that I have ever seen. But he does more than bring fresh bread from heaven when he speaks - he lives the life. He is kind, consistent, fiercely loyal and insightful. All of these qualities come out 'between the lines' in his book, *Run To Win*.

I believe that you will be encouraged, strengthened and better equipped to run your race for God by reading and reflecting on the truths presented in *Run To Win*. This book is for anyone desiring to discover what God wants them to do, how to get started doing it and how to finish well.

Bayless Conley

INTRODUCTION

*H*ave you ever wondered, "Am I doing what God wants me to do with my life?" Then, after a deep sigh, you continue to hope that what you're doing is what He wants. It's difficult to live with that type of question in your mind, especially when an answer is available.

In the following pages, you will discover some simple, yet profound, truths that will not only answer the above question, but will provide the proper perspective through which you should view life as a believer. This perspective will help you clearly see that it is a race. So many of God's children perceive life through the eyes of doubt and uncertainty, not knowing that God's will can be understood.

So what about winning? Well, everyone loves winners and I believe everyone truly desires to win. The exhilaration and the rewards of victory far outweigh losing. If you're like me, I really, really enjoy winning and really, really do not like losing. That may sound a bit one – sided and obsessive, but if you think for one moment, it's not.

A person does not open a business only to close the doors two years later, nor does a couple get married intending to file divorce papers after seven years of marriage. Students do not attend school to get bad grades, and no one seeks employment only to be fired from that employment. What I'm saying is that we desire good, to do well, to succeed; in short— we want to win. If we, in normal life situations and endeavors desire to win, how much *more* important is it when it comes to the ultimate reward, which is hearing Him say, "Well done, good and faithful servant"?

Since God's thoughts and ways are so much higher than ours, what appears as losing from a natural point of view is really winning from God's perspective. The crucifixion of Christ is a prime example of this. It appeared as though Christ was defeated and all hope was lost, but His death was the route to His victorious resurrection. So the idea of winning must be understood from God's perspective and not just our human point of view. Although our faith can be challenged and circumstances appear unfavorable this does not mean we're losing. If we are acting in accord with God's Word and plan for our lives, we are winning.

This book was written to inform, instruct and inspire you to live by God's purposes, serve people with passion and experience the prize of fulfillment now and in eternity.

Onto Chapter One!

CHAPTER 1

WE ARE IN A RACE

WE ARE IN A RACE

"**O**n your mark. Get set. Go!" This was a common announcement throughout my years of growing up. It didn't matter whether it was before breakfast or after school; whether it was at the park or in an alley with my friends, I would always race. We would race to see who was "the fastest" in our grade, on our team, or at our school. It was always an exhilarating feeling to beat someone who was older or was a respected athlete. It was a thrill to win! It gave you "bragging rights" amongst your peers.

In I Corinthians 9:24-27, the apostle Paul wrote to the church at Corinth about a race and said these words:

Do you not know that those who run in a race all run, but one receives the prize? Run in such a way that you may obtain it. And everyone who competes for the prize is temperate in all things. Now they do it to obtain a perishable crown, but we for an imperishable crown. Therefore I run thus: not with uncertainty. Thus I fight: not as one who beats the air. But I discipline my body and bring it into subjection, lest, when I have preached to others, I myself should become disqualified.

In the Bible, there are many analogies that help describe and define the Christian life. We read about comparisons to such things as salt, light, a sower, a soldier, and many more. Perhaps the primary comparison is how a Christian's life parallels that of a Greek Olympic runner in the Corinthian games. In the context of these verses, Paul is describing someone who is running a race and only one person would secure the prize.

Today, in our Olympic games, we have people who can place first and win the gold medal, second place for the silver medal, and third place for the bronze medal. However, in the Corinthian games, that was not the case; one person, and one person only, could

"When we received Jesus, we probably didn't realize that we also entered a race"

win the race. Thus it says in other translations: "...run, then for victory (Knox)[1]; and, you must run in such a way that you can get the prize," (Williams)[2]. It's important to note that the Christian race is not a race against one another, nor is it a race of one church against another church. Comparing ourselves with others is not wise (II Corinthians 10:12). This will lead us to compete rather than complement one another by helping to bring progress and improvement. Our race (and our winning that race) has to do with us continually growing and going toward spiritual maturity, living lives that are good testimonies for Jesus, and finishing the things God has called each of us to do.

The Greek runner in the Corinthian games would be rewarded very handsomely. If he won the race, the first thing that he would receive would be a pine crown, which in the Greek world was the highest possible reward; also, he would receive a red woolen ribbon that would also be placed upon him. Then he would receive a palm frond, which is also another symbol of victory. The winner would be given a hero's welcome upon his return home. Many who would win in this specific race would be moved into political roles in their particular cities, because of their new status as the winner in the games. They would receive benefits for the rest of their lives. Statues would also be erected of them– that's pretty cool! The hometown people would be so proud of the winners that they would put the image of the winners' faces on a coin, so that no one would ever forget them[3].

It's vital that you and I realize that as Christians, when we accepted Jesus into our hearts as our Savior and Lord, we not only received eternal life and have our names written in the Lamb's Book of Life, but we too entered into a race at that time.

In the following pages, I want to share some insights that are going to help you run your race in such a way that you can win. Are you interested in finding out what these things are?

We Are In A Race–Thoughts on Training to Win

1. *Meditate on the truth that as a Christian, you are in a race.*

2. *Remember that you can run (live and serve) in such a way, so as to win God's eternal prize for you.*

3. *Seek to compliment and complete fellow Christians and churches as opposed to comparing and competing with them.*

4. *Winning your race begins with growing and going towards spiritual maturity.*

CHAPTER 2

LOOK AT THE WINNER

LOOK AT THE WINNER

*F*irst and foremost, if we are going to run our race to win, we must look to Jesus. Hebrews 12:2 says, *"...and let us run with endurance the race that is set before us, looking unto Jesus, the Author and Finisher of our faith."*

You see, Jesus is the one who ran His race perfectly and finished, then sat down at the right hand of the Throne of God. We must look unto Him. That word "looking", from the original Greek language, means "to turn the eyes away from other things and fix them; to turn one's mind to a certain thing."[4] In this case, it would be Jesus.

Now when the Greek runner would be running his race, he could easily be enamored with the large number of people in the Olympic stadium, thinking, "Wow! Look at all of these people". This would definitely break his focus and concentration; or, he could be looking at the person on his left or on his right, which would cause his speed to decrease. Why would the scripture verse give us the directive to look at Jesus as our focal point? Often in these races, they would position someone who is a former winner (or even someone who had won several times) at the finish line, so the runners could see this individual and be motivated by the fact that the person is a winner.[5]

In the Olympic games, the person (to date) who has won the most Olympic medals for the United States is Michael Phelps, an American swimmer. He is the most decorated Olympian of all time with twenty-two medals (eighteen gold, two silver and two bronze), and has set numerous records along the way.[6] Although there are numerous events in the Olympic games, Michael Phelps would be a person to look at as a winner, because no one has stepped on the medal platform more than he has.[7] Jesus is the Motivator for running your race, because He is the Ultimate Winner. Christ defeated sin, death and the grave, and no one has ever succeeded in victory like He has. If you look at Him, you will win too.

I'm reminded of a time when my daughter, Brionna, was competing in her first track meet. She was running well enough to be in the heat that would qualify her to run in the state meet for her age group in the 100-yard dash. I told my daughter prior to the race, "Brionna, I'm going to be standing at the finish line. When you run, look straight at me. Just focus on me at the finish line. I'll be cheering for you." Also, I said, "Do not clench your fists when you run; keep your hands open, so that you will not run tight and constricted.

"To look unto Jesus means that we look away from everyone and everything else giving Him our undivided attention."

Lastly, do not look at the person on your left or on your right; just keep looking at Daddy. I'll be at the finish line. I'll see you there!"

The gun went off, "Bang". Brionna started off really, really well, maintaining a great pace and great stride. Then, all of a sudden, she looked at the girl next to her, who was coming up right about where she was, and Brionna began to clench her fists; and then she started running harder versus faster. The first three spots placed to go to the state finals in the 100 yard dash, but Brionna just missed it, finishing fourth. It was unfortunate, but it speaks to us of the importance of focusing on someone, and that Person upon whom we must focus, is Jesus. You might ask, "Kenneth, since Jesus is not here, present in the flesh, how do I look at Him?" Great question. Since you cannot follow Him around like the rest of the disciples were privileged to do, what does this mean?

To look unto Jesus means that we look away from everyone and everything else, giving Him our undivided attention. The ability to focus and block out distractions has always been a key quality of any athlete who has ever excelled. The ability to ignore the jeers of a hostile crowd, the intimidation of a highly skilled opponent, the pressure of the moment, or even your last mistake is invaluable. So how can you do this practically? Begin by giving your undivided and consistent attention to the reading of the Word of God. In Revelation 19:12, Jesus is called the Word of God. Look at Jesus in the Gospels of Matthew, Mark, Luke and John. Read how He treated people, His prayer life, and how He made time for children. Learn how He responded to unkind treatment and what He instructed His followers to do. You will come to know His miracles, teachings, suffering, resurrection and ascension. Whatever the main thoughts are that God speaks into your heart are what you should meditate on both day and night. As you do, your faith will be strengthened.

Another practical way to look at Jesus is to learn about Him through the lives of appointed spiritual leaders. God has given gifts of ministry to the Body of Christ (apostles, prophets, evangelists, pastors and teachers—Ephesians 4:11) for the purpose of equipping the saints for the work of ministry. One of God's key requirements for His leaders (and His people) is that we be examples of Christ by following in His footsteps (I Timothy 4:12, I Peter 5:3). This is crucial, because people closely observe the lives of God's leaders in the hope of learning from them. People may not always do what you say, but they will do what they see you do. I believe this is why the apostle Paul said, "Follow me, as I follow Christ." The lifestyle of the leader is the true message

"People may not always do what you say, but they will do what they see."

he preaches. Saint Francis of Assisi said, "Preach the gospel at all times and when necessary, use words."[8]

In addition to spiritual leaders, parents and other spiritual fathers/mothers and mentors in the faith will provide examples for us, so that we can focus on the "Jesus" we see and hear through their lives. As a matter of fact, parents are to be the first examples of God that we come in contact with. Ephesians 6:1, from the Amplified Bible, says, *"Children, obey your parents in the Lord [as His representatives], for this is just and right."*[9] I imagine the greatest complement our children could ever give us would be that they saw Christ through our lives.

Look At The Winner–Thoughts on Training to Win

1. *Purpose to look at Jesus, which means turning your eyes and mind away from other distractions and fixing them on God's Word.*

2. *Starting today, remove all possible distractions as you daily read the Bible, giving it your undivided attention.*

3. *Remember that God expects His leaders to be examples of godliness for those they are called to serve.*

4. *Define a Christ-like quality in one of your spiritual leaders/mentors that you'd like to emulate.*

CHAPTER 3

RUN YOUR RACE

RUN YOUR RACE

*A*lthough God has given us leaders and other mature believers that we can learn from, He has not given us the same race, or lane, to run in. You must run *your race*. Hebrews 12:1 says, *"Therefore we also, since we are surrounded by so great a cloud of witnesses, let us lay aside every weight, and the sin which so easily ensnares us, and let us run with endurance the race that is set before us."* One of the most well-known marathon races in the United States is the Boston Marathon. The 84th edition of this race was held on April 21, 1980. The talk of this event was a twenty-three-year-old woman named Rosie Ruiz. It appeared that she set the fastest time for a female runner in the history of the Boston Marathon, finishing in 2:31:56. This time would be the third fastest female time recorded in any marathon, but there was one problem—Rosie Ruiz did not run her race.[10]

Several runners did not recall seeing her at all during the course of the race. Ms. Ruiz did not appear in any pictures or video footage. There were two Harvard University students, John Faulkner and Sola Mahoney, who stated seeing Ms. Ruiz dart out of a crowd with less than a mile left in the race. While other suspicions were raised as to the legitimacy of her victory, an investigation was done by the Boston Athletic Association (BAA) and Ms. Ruiz was disqualified because she cheated and did not run her own race. She received no reward.[11] In the Greek games, if an athlete did not respect the rules of the race, he would be punished with a whip by one of the judges.[12]

God has set a race before each one of us. The word "set", in the original language, means "lying before".[13] Prior to the beginning of most weddings, a designated person rolls out a white runner down the aisle that the wedding party, and especially the bride, will walk on to the altar. The white runner before them provides the direction and destination to the altar.

When you believed in Jesus, there is something that God laid out before you; a course that you are supposed to run, filled with good works. Now there are other people that are next to you who are Christians, and they also have their own roads in front of them, but you can't step off of your path and run in theirs, and they can't step off of their path and run in yours. You have to run your own race. Stop reading for a moment and say these words out loud, "I will run my own race". There is an individual course divinely designed for you. Even if you are married you still have your own individual race. When you stand before Jesus Christ in Heaven, you're not going to stand before Him as husband and wife. You will not stand before Christ together as a family; you will stand before Him as an individual, to give account for your life here on earth (II Corinthians 5:10). If you're married, you serve and you co-labor together, but each of you still have individual works that God has prepared for you both that will help people and glorify Him.

"...you will stand before God as an individual to give account for your life here on earth."

Psalm 33:15 says that God fashions our hearts individually. You are not a manufactured, assembly-line product, but a unique individual, fearfully and wonderfully made by God. Out of the 7.3 billion people on the

44

planet, there is no one else like you. With all the people that have come and gone, there is no one else like you; nor will there ever be anyone like you after you. Think about it, you are not just one in a million, but one in billions, made by the Creator Himself.

Listen, God has given you gifts: He has given you talents, skills, abilities, a wonderful personality, intelligence, strength and wisdom. All of these things, compiled together, are to be used in the running of your race. There is no one in God's kingdom that is bankrupt of potential, my friend. Every child of God has been given much; and to whom much is given, much is required. You have a race to run…you have a destiny to fulfill…run *your* race!

You were born an original, thus you should not die a copy. Foregoing whom God has made you, and the gifts He has given you, to try to be like someone else will prove to be fruitless.

Wishing you were someone else, or coveting another's gifts and abilities, denies you and the

"Wishing you were someone else, or coveting another's gifts and abilities, denies you and the rest of us the opportunity to appreciate God's grace in your life."

rest of us the opportunity to appreciate God's grace in your life. Attempting to run in another person's lane will drain you of energy, creativity, peace and much more.

In II Chronicles 26:16-21, we read of Uzziah, the tenth king of Judah. He allowed pride to overtake his heart and attempted to run someone else's race instead of his own. Let's look at his story. After Uzziah became powerful, his pride led to his downfall. He was unfaithful to the Lord his God and entered the temple of the Lord to burn incense on the altar of incense. Azariah the priest, with eight other courageous priests of the Lord, followed him in. They confronted King Uzziah and said:

It is not right for you, Uzziah, to burn incense to the Lord. That is for the priests, the descendants of Aaron, who have been consecrated to burn incense. Leave the sanctuary, for you have been unfaithful; and you will not be honored by the Lord God. Uzziah, who had a censer in his hand ready to burn incense, became angry. While he was raging at the priests in their presence before the incense altar in the Lord's temple, leprosy broke out on his forehand. When Azariah the chief priest and all the other priests looked at him, they saw that he had leprosy on his forehand, so they hurried him out. Indeed, he himself was eager to leave because the Lord had afflicted him. King Uzziah had leprosy until the day he died. He lived in a separate house – leprous and banned from

the temple of the Lord... (II Chronicles
26: 16-21 NIV)

In the Old Testament, there were three primary offices: the prophet, the priest and the
king. Each were called to function and fulfill a specific role in serving God by serving
His people. Uzziah was a king; this was his
calling. He had a lane he was designed to run
in, but pride made him think he could run in
the priests' lanes. His unwillingness to heed
the counsel of the prophets opened him up to
God's judgment. So, the lesson is to remain
humble, stay in our lanes, and don't let pride
tempt us to do something that we are not called
by God to do.

This is why it is imperative that we look at
Jesus, because sometimes we choose to look at
someone else. Imagine seeing someone running
in your neighborhood. He or she has the most

recent Nike® apparel and running glasses, a perfect stride, and is looking fit. This person just looks good. You have a moment of inspiration, so you put on your old, cut-off jean shorts, your favorite shirt and your Chuck Taylor Converse. You take off from your front door in a blaze of glory, thinking you're the Nike® runner you were looking at earlier, but ten minutes later you realize you are not. You don't look like this person, nor do you run like him. You run your race; let the Nike® runner run his.

I taught a young lady in Sunday school and was privileged to officiate her wedding. Her name was Andrea Anderson (now Andrea Bolder). In 2000, she ran for the United States in the Women's 4x400 gold medal team. Here's a quote from Andrea, relative to this point:

"I believe that God gives each of us talents, but it's up to the individual to take those talents and use them to make the very best you. With the right tools, hard work and a bit of motivation, you can maximize your talents."

I am sure many of us would agree that we have been underachieving. There is so much more that we have inside of us to give, but we're looking at the charismatic runners next to us, thinking that they have so much more than us, and it's just not true.

You have your own race. God did not place you in this race, or give you the tools that you need, so that you couldn't win. He does not set us up for failure. On the contrary, He sets us up perfectly to succeed.

Run Your Race–Thoughts on Training to Win

1. *Close your eyes and imagine standing alone before Jesus, as He asks about your life on earth.*

2. *Realize your lane is filled with good works to serve others, prepared beforehand by the Lord.*

3. *Learn from Uzziah by remaining in your calling and maintaining a humble heart (II Chronicles 26:16-21).*

4. *Consider that God has fashioned you individually, and being yourself shows the uniqueness of His grace in your life.*

CHAPTER 4

FINDING YOUR LANE

FINDING YOUR LANE

$\mathcal{I}$n every short or long-distance race, each runner is assigned to a numeric lane. A runner is not allowed to choose lane 1, 2, 6 or 7; the lane is assigned. God has assigned our lanes for us to run in, based on His gifts and designated calling, which reflect His divine wiring within us.

So how do you know your lane? Before I share my personal experience and some ways to discover *your* lane, let me say, YOU CAN KNOW THIS. Many times we are tricked into thinking that God's plan for our lives is a mysterious, distant concept that we cannot know, yet the Bible states that we can understand the will of the Lord (Ephesians 5:17). This means we can possess this knowledge so we can do it–so we can run our race. My story...

Very early in my walk with the Lord, I began to sense that God was calling me to preach His Word, but I wasn't sure and really wanted to be certain. I began to ask other ministers this question, "How do you know if God has called you to preach?" I heard a variety of responses, but didn't receive any concrete answers that satisfied my thirst to know. One response that I vividly recall from one pastor was, "You just know that you know". Then he quoted I Corinthians 9:16, which says, *"Woe is me if I do not preach the gospel."* While I believe this response came from a sincere heart, it still left me with the question I initially asked. I know this type of question is very common, because each person wants to know what God has called and gifted him/her to do while on earth. So, if you were to ask me, "How do I find what God has called me to do? How do I discover my purpose? How do I know my lane?" This would be my answer.

1) Ask:

The best way to obtain this answer is by asking the One who has called you to run your race. The great apostle Paul asked Jesus, "Lord, what do you want me to do?" (Acts 9:6). It was a simple prayer,

"The best way to obtain this answer is by asking the One who has called you to run your race."

and God obviously answered him. Yet in writings to the churches at Ephesus and Colosse, Paul gave some inspired instruction on what to pray for God's answer to these questions of our hearts. The following prayers are ones that I've prayed, and still do to this day, for family, others, and myself. They are written in the first person, so you could pray them, too.

> …Father of glory, may you give to [me] the spirit of wisdom and revelation in the knowledge of Him [Jesus], the eyes of [my] understanding being enlightened; that [I] may know what is the hope of His calling… (Ephesians 1:17-18).

> …[I] ask that [I] may be filled with the knowledge of His will in all wisdom and spiritual understanding; that [I] may walk worthy of [You] Lord, fully pleasing [You], being fruitful in every good work and increasing in the knowledge of God… (Colossians 1:9-10).

Please know that as you pray these prayers, God is faithful to answer them.

2) Find yourself in the Word:

Studying the Bible is the way we can know anything about God, including His plans for humanity and for our lives as individuals. It is His chosen and pri-

mary method of revealing Himself. Since God is Life, His

"The way we know anything about God, His plans for humanity and for our lives can be found in His Word – the Bible."

words are living and if we seek Him and His plan for our lives, He will not be silent; He is willing to speak to our hearts. Let's read about an experience in the life of Jesus:

So He came to Nazareth, where He had been brought up. And as His custom was, He went into the synagogue on the Sabbath day, and stood up to read. And He was handed the book of the prophet Isaiah. And when He had opened the

*book, He found the place where it was
written:*

*"The Spirit of the Lord is upon Me,
because He has anointed Me to preach
the gospel to the poor; He has sent Me to
heal the brokenhearted, to proclaim liberty to the captives and recovery of sight
to the blind, to set at liberty those who
are oppressed; to proclaim the acceptable year of the Lord" (Luke 4:16-19).*

In this passage, Jesus was reading from
the prophet Isaiah, but was really reading
about what He was called and anointed to
do. If you will make it your personal habit
to open up God's book and read, you will
find that what was written thousands of years
ago will speak to your heart today. This happened to me as I prayed about His calling for
my life. God spoke clearly and repeatedly to

me about running in the lane of preaching
and teaching the Word. One verse He used,
regarding the latter, was Exodus 35:34.
Moses was speaking to the children of Israel
about a builder named Bezalel. When I read
this verse, I knew it was the Lord speaking
to me, saying, *"And He has put in his heart
the ability to teach…"* God is no respecter of
persons; seek Him about His gifts and calling,
and He will show you.

3) An Inward Witness:

There are many ways in which God can
communicate with us. When it comes to our
salvation, which is based on our relationship
with Him, let's consider these words from
Romans 8:16; *"The Spirit Himself bears witness with our spirit that we are children of
God."* One of the common tactics of the devil
is to make us doubt that God is real and that

our salvation experience was genuine. Would you agree with me that there is nothing more important than a person being born-again into God's family? Nothing can compare with this on the scales of eternity. With that being said, the way God has chosen to assure us that we are actually His children is by the inward witness; an inward knowing. The Holy Spirit makes it known to our spirit (the real you) that you are God's child. The devil will always shoot thoughts of doubt at your mind, but the inward witness in your heart will always prevail. God is Spirit, therefore He communicates and confirms His salvation and *your calling* in your spirit. It's called the inward witness.

4) Strong Desire:

We often think that the thing we are the most opposed to and like the least is what God will choose for us to do to serve Him.

Yet, the opposite is true. God gives us a desire to actually want to do the thing He has called us to do. This is an unmistakable quality of knowing which lane you're called to run in. Paul said, in I

"God gives us a desire to actually want to do the thing He's called us to do."

Timothy 3:1, *"This is a faithful saying: If a man desires the position of a bishop, he desires a good work."* Desire is mentioned twice in this verse and before any leadership qualifications are given. Desire could be an area in which God is communicating to you that may be overlooked while discovering your lane. God is smarter than we are and knows that the desire for something must be alive in us first before we'll begin to pursue and do it.

I want to share two more verses that have really helped me on this topic of desire. The first one is Psalm 37:4; *"Delight yourself also in the Lord, and He will give you the desires of your heart."* This is one of my life verses, because Christ became my delight (and still is) when He saved me, so this verse automatically reignited this within my heart. In the Strong's Exhaustive Concordance of the Bible, the word "delight" means to be soft or pliable, to delight self. This has to do with the positions and postures of our hearts before God; a willingness to yield to Him. Once this is incorporated into our lives, then the "...and He shall give you the desires of your heart" comes next. There are two ways to understand the latter part of this great verse, and they are:

1. As you delight yourself in the Lord, He will give, or put, His desires in your heart.
2. God will grant you those heart desires that are consistent with His will for your life.

If you received fresh insight from Psalm 37:4, you will definitely get excited about this next verse, which will actually bring some connection to what God does in hearts, relating to desire.

[Not in your own strength] for it is God Who is all the while effectually at work in you [energizing and creating in you the power and desire], both to will and to work for His good pleasure and satisfaction and delight (Philippians 2:13, Amplified).

I came across this verse at a time when I wasn't clear which lane to run in (but knew for certain that I wanted to run in the service of God and others). It was like sweet music to my soul, because I knew that whatever God had for me, He would create the desire for it and the power to do it within me. This blessed me beyond measure, because I did not want to get into something that wasn't from God, nor try to manufacture something on my own. He does the work through your desire for Him.

5) Vision — what do you see?

One of the more commonly used verses related to vision is found in Proverbs 29:18; *"Where there is no vision, the people perish..."* I've mainly heard this verse applied to church, in corporate and even in national context; but the powerful truth in this verse applies to you as an individual. The word vision does not exclusively apply to our physical ability to see, but to a spiritual sight called revelation. This is when God reveals something to you inwardly– in your spirit.

There are things God shows us individually and specifically that are unique to the race that He has called each of us to run. Some people see the homeless and impoverished and are moved with compassion; while others see the lack of structure and systems in an organization and are stirred to lend their organi-

"There are things God shows us individually and specifically that are unique to the race that He's called each of us to run."

zational skills or strategic thinking to meet needs; others see a void of leadership, direction and vision and are moved to want to help, etc. When you see something, you see what's wrong or what's not working – you see what could be. This brings about frustration and can lead to a bad attitude and verbal complaints if you're not careful. Your frustration rises within you because no one seems to see what is clear and obvious to you. Understand that everyone does not see what you see. What's going on? God is showing you what's wrong, or what can be, so you can be a part of the solution to make things better. What God opens *your* eyes to see is for the purpose of transforming your family, community, church, organization and the world.

6) Fruitfulness in Service:

"You did not choose Me, but I chose you and appointed you that you should go and bear fruit, and that your fruit should remain, that whatever you ask the Father in My name He may give you," *(John 15:16).*

Imagine walking into a vast apple orchard. You're amazed at the numerous trees, full of ripe, delicious apples. As you pass through the orchard, your attention is drawn to an intriguing sight–a tree that has no fruit on its branches. This sight is baffling, because it's an anomaly among the other trees filled with fruit.

As you walk away, trying to figure out the mystery of the fruitless tree, you are puzzled at another tree unlike any other in the immense orchard. All the apples on this tree are rotten, unable to be harvested and sold to the market. The tree had obviously produced, but what was produced did not last, it did not remain.

We've been chosen and ordained by God to be productive and that productivity would remain, bearing eternal fruit. This occurs by us doing what God has placed within us, and put before us to do. When you are in your *"When you are in your lane their will be fruit and when you're out of your lane there will be frustration."* lane, there will be fruit and when you're out of your lane, there will be frustration. When you are where He chooses and you are faithful, you will blossom. (Numbers 17:1-8).

7) Confirmation of Church Leadership:

Leaders in God's church are normal people like you and me. These men and women are running in their respective lanes to build up the church to reach the world for Christ. The Holy Spirit gives leaders in the Body of Christ oversight (Acts 20:28), and because of this role, He also gives them *insight*. Both are needed to properly lead, equip and care for His flock (Hebrews 13:17). When you are committed to a local church (which is God's plan for every believer), you place yourself in submission under the chosen leadership.

As you faithfully serve and relate with your leaders, there are things they will see in you that you may not even see in yourself. You don't need a church leader to tell you God's purpose for your life,

> *"As you faithfully serve and relate with your leaders, there are things they will see in you that you may not even see in yourself."*

because the Lord is more than capable of doing that. However, a leader may be able to confirm what's already in you, and counsel you on preparation, direction and more. This will provide confidence in you for what the Lord is doing in, and will do through you.

Finding Your Lane–Thoughts on Training to Win

1. *Settle it in your heart that you can know and understand God's plan (lane) for your life.*

2. *Find your lane by committing to do the following:*
   - *Ask God*
   - *Find yourself in the Word*
   - *Acknowledge the inward witness*
   - *Follow strong desire*
   - *Receive revelation/vision from God*
   - *Assess where you're fruitful in serving*
   - *Get confirmation from church leadership.*

CHAPTER 5

HOW TO RUN MY RACE

HOW TO RUN MY RACE

$\mathcal{U}$pon discovering the lane you have been designed and gifted for, and now called to run in, you need to know the "how". Thankfully, the Bible is not silent on this aspect of our race. Read on.

Number one: travel light. Hebrews 12:1 says, " *Lay aside every weight and the sin which so easily ensnares us.*" During the ancient times of the games in Greece, runners would train and run in the nude. (Thank God times have changed!) The runners would wear their clothes all day, but would strip down and put oil on their bodies and then dust themselves off with sand. The oil and the sand together would regulate their body temperatures, protect them from the rays of the sun, and also help them when their trainers would hit them with a stick. The trainer would only do this if the runner didn't train correctly. So the runners would take off everything that would hinder them from running.[14] Weights are defined as bulk or mass.[15] Sometimes we are carrying bulk in our lives; we have things that create more mass in our lives and they weigh us down. Due to being "weighed down" it becomes ever more difficult to run our Christian races. We become fatigued, not realizing our dire need to relinquish the excess baggage. Weights are not necessarily sin; they are things that don't help us. If something is not helping you, then it is hindering you. You have to be the one to determine what you need

"if something is not helping you, then it is hindering you."

to let go of or take off. Could it be putting down the remote control? An unhealthy relationship? Negative Speech? It could be something very innocent, but for you, it is a weight and it pulls you down. May God help us and show us those things that are weighing us down. Paul said, in 1 Corinthians 6:12, *"All things are lawful for me, but all things are not helpful."* We must be able to distinguish between the two.

Then it says, *"Lay aside 'the sin' "*; not the sins, plural, but the sin. Normally there is one area of weakness that seems to plague us. The author says lay

> *"Normally, there is one area of weakness that seems to plague us."*

aside the sin; that thing, that weakness, that annoying propensity that we continue to repeat. Whether it is anger, lust or gossip, you can lay it aside. It will not help you run your race the way that God has designed and planned for you to do.

The picture of "the sin" in Hebrews 12:1 is a long robe that clings to your legs, making it very difficult for you to walk in because it is wrapping itself around your legs. This is what it is talking about when it says "the sin that so easily besets us".[16] It's not difficult, nor is it hard; it's easy. You can effortlessly slip into it.

> *"You may think it is impossible to cease and desist because you have repeatedly fallen, but YOU HAVE THE POWER TO LAY IT DOWN."*

If you cannot put your finger on what the sin may be, God will show you what it is, if you sincerely want to lay it aside. You may think it is impossible to cease and desist, because you have repeatedly fallen, but YOU HAVE THE POWER TO LAY IT DOWN.

I'm intrigued when I read in John 8 about the woman that was caught in adultery, then brought to Jesus by the Scribes and Pharisees. Jesus tells this woman in John 8:14, *"Go and sin no more"*. That woman had not been born-again, thus she did not have the nature of God in her and was not filled with the power of God's Spirit, yet Jesus said to her, "Go and sin and no more", which means she was able to make a conscious choice to no longer perform the sin of adultery.

Note what God said to Cain in Genesis 4:6-7:

Why are you angry? And why has your countenance fallen? If you do well, will you not be accepted? And if you do not do well, sin lies at the door. And its desire is for you, but YOU SHOULD RULE OVER IT.

Sin does not have to overpower you. I know that the pleasure and pull of sin can be over-powering to us mentally, but the grace of God is greater than any and every sin. Call on God, and He will help you to be the conqueror that you already are.

Number two: adopt a "marathon mindset". This is why Hebrews 12:1 says:

Therefore we also, since we are sur-rounded by so great a cloud of witnesses, let us lay aside every weight, and the sin which so easily ensnares us, and let us run with endurance the race that is set before us.

The word "endurance" from the Greek lan-guage means constancy, perseverance, contin-uance, bearing up, steadfast, holding out, and patient endurance. It describes the capacity to continue to bear up under difficult cir-cumstances, not with a passive complacency, but with a hopeful fortitude that actively resists weariness and defeat.[17] This quality is specifically mentioned to relate to how we, as Christians, must run our own races.

Jesus is our Ultimate Example of endurance, as He persevered through every false accusation leading up to the crucifixion and the cross itself, until He finally cried out *"It is finished!"* (John 19:30). Betrayal, rejection, sleep deprivation, flogging, asphyxiation and the rejection of His Father and the Holy Spirit did not stop Jesus. The context of this verse provides two specific applications of endurance as we run our races.

The first is hostility from sinners (Hebrews 12:3). These Jewish Christians were in the middle of being persecuted for their faith in Christ as they heard this letter of exhortation. Christianity had become more than a Jewish sect, and had spread throughout the world. As this was realized by the Roman Emperor Nero, and other emperors following him,

Jewish Christians were no longer given privileges they had once experienced before. These believers were suffering persecution, lost property (Hebrews 10:32-34) and were wavering in their faith in Christ.

The thought of returning to the practices of Judaism became an attractive option for them, as they considered the persecution of their countrymen. Not everyone will support and applaud your service at church, in your community or in living a life that coincides with biblical values.

"People who do not want to change will persecute the transformation Christ has brought in your life."

People who do not want to change will persecute the transformation Christ has brought in your life. Don't allow this to stop you.

This race of faith is not a sprint. You don't start out and then, in ten seconds, days, or even years, finish; this is a long-distance run. This is not something that happens all at once when you have a deep revelation of God and can quote several Bible verses in a short period of time. No, it's not like that, my friend. It takes time in this walk with God, and He is not in a rush. The plans and purposes of God for your life roll themselves out day after day, week after week, month after month, and year after year. His plans for you are revealed to you over time. Rome wasn't built in one day, and the destiny of God for your life will not be accomplished in one day either, so you and I must develop the mindset of a marathon runner.

There will be seasons when the wind is behind your back and you will experi-

"There will be seasons when the wind is behind your back and you will experience the momentum of God's Spirit."

ence the momentum of God's Spirit. Although you're working hard, progress will happen in a more timely manner and with ease; but there will be seasons when you're running into the wind and will experience resistance. The devil cannot stop you, but he will certainly tempt you and attempt to hinder you. This is not the time to stop because of the wind, but to lean forward and continue to run. This is where your muscles are built. It's been said that genius is one percent inspiration and ninety-nine percent perspiration.

When you run a sprint, you're trying to get to the end as quickly as you can. When you run a marathon, the goal is not to get there as quickly as you can, but simply to get there, to finish.

Our Leadership College at Cottonwood hosted a 1K/5K run/walk and I participated in this inaugural event. I had experience running sprints before, but had never run a distance race competitively or recreationally. Consequently, I had never trained for a 5K, which is 3.1 miles.

Moreover, I was unclear on the strategy of how to run that particular race.

When I arrived at the starting line, I saw all these people looking at their watches and running in place. My thought was, "I don't know what they are doing, but anyway." Suddenly the gun went off and I was like a horse right out of the starting gate. "Ooh yeah, ooh yeah. I feel this." I was out there in front, coming around the corner and then, all of a sudden, something weird happened. My quadriceps (front thigh muscles) started getting really, really tight; and then I got a pain on my left side.

One by one, people started passing me. Whoosh, whoosh, whoosh. Then the most humbling event happened to me since I began playing sports in the third grade. I was running as best I could, and this short, young, thin girl came flying right past me, but that's not all. That embarrassment was getting me prepared for the worst! A man pushing his child in a stroller ran past me, then turned and said to me, "Come on, man!" I couldn't believe this! In my exasperated state, I thought, "Lord, it is enough! Take me home!"

You can't run a marathon with a sprinter's mentality. The next time we had the 1K/5K run/walk, I approached the race with a distance mentality rather than a sprint mentality. I didn't try to beat anybody in the beginning, I just waited; I let people pass me up. Later on, I began to pass by the people who had earlier passed me by. It was a different strategy based on a different mindset.

I guess you could say I graduated to more of a true long-distance race, the Long Beach Marathon. Over two hundred and fifty people from our church trained for sixteen weeks in preparation to either run the full marathon (26.2 miles), ride a bike, or either run or walk the half-marathon (13.1 miles). Since this was my first time running in a "long-distance race", I thought it would be wise if I started out running the half-marathon as opposed to the full marathon.

Every Saturday we trained together, increasing our mileage week by week, then decreasing it as "race day" drew closer. Each of us was responsible to train on our own two to three times per week, thirty to forty-five minutes each time. About eight or nine weeks into our training, I started to get a pain on the outer part of my left knee. I've been involved in organized sports since third grade, all through college, and to the present recreationally. Over the years, my main sport has been basketball, which is a fast-pace game requiring a high amount of running, jumping and lateral movement. I never experienced knee problems while playing, nor did I ever have this type of knee pain.

When I told my running coach and the physical therapist about the pain, it was concluded that what I was experiencing had to do with my iliotibial band. This ligament runs down the outside of the thigh and attaches to the knee, helping to stabilize and move the joint. When the pain would come during training, I would walk for a moment, try to run, but would eventually have to stop. I was frustrated having to walk as others were running past me. Despite the pain, I would attempt to run, only having to stop once again.

Race day finally came. All was going well; I didn't start off too fast, found a good pace, and established my breathing rhythm, but on mile number five...you guessed it. My knee began to hurt as it did in training. "Oh no!" I thought. "I don't want to walk 8.1 miles; I've

trained too hard." This was the thought when-
ever the pain happened, but I could not stop. I
couldn't accept
this—I had to endure.

*"The marathon mindset is
one of endurance."*

I walked some, tried
to run, prayed, confessed healing scriptures,
called on the name of Jesus, and then began to
run again. I had to alter my form, decrease my
speed, but I was running. The pain was not as
intense, so I could still run. There were three
times during the last 3.1 miles where I felt no
pain and was able to sprint, so I had a great finish.

The marathon mindset is one of endurance.
During those times when you feel like giving
up–just keep running. Just keep putting one
foot in front of the other and keep on going.
The pain and the hindrances will dissipate, and
God will strengthen you to finish.

The second area that requires endurance has
to do with God's chastening (discipline) through

rebuke, correction and instruction (Hebrews 12:7). Chastening is a part of God's role as the Father of our spirits. When we did something wrong as a child, our parents or legal guardians would correct us by spanking. [This practice is not as prevalent today as it used to be.] We felt some pain due to our smart mouths, bad attitudes, or disobedience. Well, God the Father does not spank you with a belt, nor does He yell and scream at you. He corrects us in our spirits with His Word and by the Holy Spirit. The reason that we must endure the Lord's discipline is because it is not joyful, but rather painful. It causes us to disregard and let go of unfruitful (unproductive) areas of our lives. If we are trained by God's discipline, it will produce the peaceful fruit of righteousness.

"I believe the greatest motive for you and I during times of discipline is the truth that He loves us."

I believe the greatest motivation for you and I during times of discipline is the truth that He loves us. God has no selfish motives, anger, or feelings of embarrassment about us. He just loves us so much that He wants us to be more like Him.

Number three: be accountable. Although each one of us has our own race set before him/her, the running of our races will not be done in isolation. Proverbs 18:1 admonishes us to not isolate our-

"...the running of our race is not to be done in isolation."

selves, stating that a man who does this rages against all wise judgment. In Ecclesiastes 4:9, it says that two are better than one. When Jesus sent out His disciples, He sent them two by two, which means that you will have to serve under and alongside other people, thus the need for accountability.

In Galatians 2:1-2, Paul says:

Then after fourteen years I went up again to Jerusalem with Barnabas, and also took Titus with me. And I went up by revelation, and communicated to them that gospel which I preach among the Gentiles, but privately to those who were of reputation, lest by any means I might run, or had run, in vain.

Let me repeat that phrase again; *"lest by any means I might run, or had run, in vain."*

Paul did something to ensure that he was running the right way and not in vain. In the Weymouth's Translation, verse two says; *"And I put before them the gospel which I proclaim among the Gentiles. I did this in private to the leaders of the church for fear that I was running or should have run in vain."*[18] Taylor's translation says it this way, *"I talked privately to the leaders of the church, so that they would all understand just what I had been teaching and I hoped they would agree that it was right."*[19] Wow! That last sentence is astounding, when we consider Paul's credentials. Although he was anointed and greatly used by God, he did not see himself above being accountable. Paul preached the message of Christ to the Gentiles, but recognized that he needed to consult with the church leaders. He didn't want to do it in public, but wanted to do it in private and share with them what he had been doing in his ministry. Paul wanted to ensure that what he was doing was acceptable. If it was not, then he wanted to be corrected. He wanted to run well, not in vain.

By his example, Paul teaches a very clear truth about accountability and that is, "It goes up". This means that each person is responsible for his

"Paul teaches a very clear truth about accountability and that is, "It goes up"."

actions and must be willing to communicate regarding what he has, or has not done to the person who is directly above him organization-ally–the person who delegated responsibility and authority to him in the first place. Paul went to leadership, instead of the leaders coming to him. Therefore, accountability requires initia-tive, honesty and responsibility. It is a leader's right to ask you questions about what you're doing, but many choose to rely on the leader initiating this type of dialogue as opposed to the former.

If we ever think that we are exempt from being accountable, then that is our clue that we have a problem. We are not going to run our race the way God intended us to run our race and win. I have told my three daughters that no matter how high you go, or what level of authority that you may be given, you will always be accountable to someone. Where does that accountability begin? It begins with being accountable to your spouse, to your parents (if you're under their roof) and to the other leaders in your life. You need accountability, and so do I. This is why Proverbs 11:14 says, *"...in the multitude of counselors there is safety"*.

What if there is no counsel? Then there is danger. We need the input of others, because we all have blind spots. Sometimes there are things that are going on with our attitudes, actions or our words that we don't see. So, we need others who love us enough to help us stay accountable, so we don't run our races in vain. I have learned through experience and observation that a submissive attitude is essential for accountability. Without this position of heart, a person can miss out on the open doors of opportunities that God has for him to be a blessing and to be blessed.

I'm reminded of a man named Apollos; the Bible says some very impressive things about him. He was an eloquent man, mighty in the scriptures: instructed in the way of the Lord; fervent in spirit; spoke and taught accurately the things of the Lord; and spoke boldly in the synagogue (Acts 18: 24-26). Apollos was obviously gifted and already being used of God, and due to a submissive and accountable heart, God was able to use him even more. The Bible says that he *greatly* helped those who had believed through grace (Acts 18:27). Let this truth on accountability become a practice in your life and watch how many people will be greatly helped by God through you.

How to Run My Race–Thoughts on Training to Win

1. Ask yourself, "What weights in my life need to be laid aside?"

2. Understand that sin does not have dominion over you, because of Christ's work on the cross.

3. Remember that a "marathon mindset" equates to the qualities of endurance, consistency, and perseverance.

4. Be determined to endure God's discipline in your life, in order to yield the peaceable fruit of righteousness.

5. Practice accountability from the bottom-up.

CHAPTER 6

WIN

WIN

"You were born to win, but to be a winner, you must plan to win, prepare to win and expect to win." – Zig Ziglar

"Winning is not everything, but wanting to win is." – Vince Lombardi

We must run to win. In 1 Corinthians 9:24-25, from The Message, it says, *"You've all been to the stadium and seen the athletes race. Everyone runs; one wins. **Run to win.** All good athletes train hard. They do it for a gold medal that tarnishes and fades.*

You're after one that's gold eternally." The Greek runner did not prepare himself and go through rigorous training in order to be a participant. He didn't run to participate; he ran to *win*. As followers of Jesus Christ, we're to do likewise. Here are some areas to help you and I run to win:

1). We need to continue obeying the truth of God's Word. In The Message, in Galatians 5:7, Paul says, *"You ran well. Who hindered you from obeying the truth?* In essence, Paul was saying, "See, you were running well, you were doing good, but somewhere along the way, you were hindered from obeying the truth." . Let us not put a question mark where God has placed a period. Think about it; what can we do in our relationship with our Heavenly Father that supersedes obedience?

The word "hinder", in the aforementioned verse, literally means, "to cut into"[20]. The picture is this; you are running along in your lane on a track, and someone in the next lane crosses over from his lane and cuts into your lane–that's dangerous. This person could have hurt you, himself, or others. At the very least, it definitely slows down your forward progress. In Galatians, there was a group called Judaizers, and they were trying to get these believers in Galatia to think they had to apply the laws of Moses in their lives in order for them to actually be saved. They undermined the doctrinal truth that salvation was by grace through faith in Christ alone, and it's the Holy Spirit who does the work inside of us. It's not us trying to work and make ourselves better, but it's God in us working to do those things that bring Him pleasure. Our obedience is essential.

2). If we are going to win, we must then strive for the prize. In 1 Corinthians 9:25, it says,

"And everyone who competes for the prize". The key thought of that scriptural phrase means to "agonize"[21]. This is not saying that God wants us to be anxious about the races that He has given us to run, nor is it saying that He wants us to agonize over whether or not we are doing everything perfectly right or wrong. I believe what is being communicated to us through that word "agonize", in the original language, is that God wants us to simply put forth a full effort.

Give it your all in living out your Christian life in this race of faith. Don't live a half-hearted, lukewarm life; serve God with all of your heart, mind, soul and strength. The scripture says, in Romans 12:11, *"...not lagging in diligence, fervent in spirit serving the Lord"*. Your spirit should be on fire with the privilege of knowing God and the opportunity to serve Him. It's not because you're positioned in front of people; even if you are behind the scenes and no one sees you or knows your name–you should be on fire for God. You're motivated because what you are doing is part of what you were created to do and is part of your course. So whether you are changing diapers, counseling youth, designing software, or running a business, if it's in your course, do it with all of your heart. Give it a full effort. It's not God's plan to endow you with potential and not have it released to help others. Give one hundred percent and you will see yourself go forward in maturity and growth.

In Illustrations Unlimited by James S. Hewett, I read a story about some minstrels who lived in a far country and who traveled from town to town, playing music to make a living. They had been doing well, but times were hard; there was little money for common folk to come to hear the minstrels, even though their fees were small.

Attendance had been falling off, so early one evening, the group met to discuss their plight. "I see no reason for opening tonight," one said. "To make things even worse than they already are, it is starting to snow. Who will venture out on a night like this?" "I agree," another disheartened singer said. "Last night, we performed for just a handful. Fewer will come tonight. Why not give back their meager fees and cancel the concert? No one can expect us to go on when just a few are in the audience." "How can anyone do his best for so few?" a third inquired. Then he turned to another sitting beside him and asked "What do you think?" The man to whom he addressed the question was older than the others. He looked straight at his troupe and replied "I know you are discouraged. I am too. But we have a responsibility to those who might come. We will go on. And we will do the best job of which we are capable. It is not the fault of those who come that others do not. They should not be punished with less than the best we can give." Heartened by his words, the minstrels went ahead with their show; they never performed better. When the show was over, and the small audience had gone, the old man called his troupe to him. In his hand was a note, handed to him by one of the audience members just before the doors closed behind him. "Listen to this, my friends!" Excitement in his tone made them turn to him in anticipation. Slowly, the old man read: "Thank you for a beautiful performance." It was signed very simply "Your King". There may be times when we serve hundreds and thousands, or, like the minstrels in the story, just a few. The key is in remembering that we really serve Jesus – the King.[22]

Colossians 3:23-24 marvelously accentuates this truth: *"And whatever you do, do it heartily, as to the Lord and not to men, knowing the reward of the inheritance; for you serve the Lord Christ."*

3). Another point that can help us run to win is to have a self-controlled lifestyle. First Corinthians 9:25 says, *"And everyone who competes for the prize is temperate (self-controlled) in all things."* Now that word "temperate", from the Greek language, is where we obtain our English word "abstinence". Temperance was not confined to one thing or one class of things, but applies to every indulgence that would render the body weak[23]. I would like to talk a minute about that word "abstinence", because the most common usage or application of that word has to do with sexuality.

In the world and culture that we live in today, we are truly bombarded with sexual images. Is this true or false, or am I living in a different world? They're everywhere, and our young people are being pressured into sexual activities probably more than any other previous generation has ever experienced. The word "abstinence" is a powerful Bible word; it's a God word, and I want to encourage those of you who are young to keep yourselves sexually pure. The thought of remaining a virgin in today's

"God does not require anything more from us than our obedience."

world may seem archaic, but it is both possible and do-able despite opposing opinions. This would include sexual experimentations that may not be the full act of intercourse, but are definite gray areas. If you are a single young lady, I admonish you to not give up anything to any boy because he is "all that". You don't have to lose your virginity; you can keep it if you choose to. I don't care how popular a boy may be, or how good he looks. I don't care if he is muscular, has a great smile and a twinkle in his eye. Refuse his advances for sexual intercourse. *"I charge you, O daughters of Jerusalem, do not stir up nor awaken love until it pleases"* (Song of Solomon 8:4).

To single young men, realize this: it does not make you a man to conquer girls sexually. This is not God's standard for manhood. What makes you a man is living for God: having integrity, being responsible, being accountable and serving others. I remember that locker room talk. Guys would say, "Yah, I was with this girl and I was with that girl"; then you find out later it wasn't true. Guys were trying to be something that they weren't, in order to make an impression

> *"Stand up and do not be afraid if you stand out. It's ok to stand-alone when you stand for God."*

because of peer pressure. Stand up, and do not be afraid if you stand out. It's okay to stand alone when you stand for God.

For those of you who are single, you don't need to engage yourself sexually because you are an adult and you have needs. Everyone has needs; God knows you have needs. However, God gives us guidelines in His Word; keep yourself pure (II Timothy 2:22). The Holy Spirit will give you power over your flesh and over its passions (Romans 8:5-11; Galatians 5:16-26). He will help you.

If you're married, love the one you're with. You have a covenant, because of your vow before God and to your spouse, keep your word. If you say, "I love you", then love him/her and only love him/her. Do not flirt or have another mister or mistress on the side. The grass may look greener on the other side, but it's all artificial. It looks greener, but it's not real. The person you are married to is a gift from God; see him or her as such. Why would you give up a prudent woman that's from the

Lord for some other woman who has no commitment to you? Let us abstain and live in such a way that pleases the Lord.

First Corinthians 9:25 said to be temperate in "all things", not just in sexual issues. Self-control should be applied to spending, eating, hobbies and to any area that appears to be out of control. If we are out of control, God will help us.

"Self control should be applied to spending, eating, hobbies and to any area that appears to be out of control."

The Greek sage and writer Epictetus quoted the requisite preparations for someone who would want to win the prize. He said:

You have to live on unpleasant food; You have to abstain from all delicacies; You have to exercise at prescribed times whether it's hot or whether it's cold; You have to drink nothing cool; You cannot have any wine, and you have to put yourself under a pugilist (which is our word for boxer)[24].

In other words, someone who wants to win a running race has to train with somebody who's a boxer and take that kind of physical discipline. It is important that we live disciplined lifestyles, because they are the roads to destiny.

Then, we need to forget those things that are behind and reach forward to the things that are ahead. Paul said, in Philippians 3:13-14, "... *forgetting those things which are behind and reaching forward to those things which are ahead, I press toward the goal for the prize of the upward call of God in Christ Jesus.*" What was Paul speaking of when he said "forgetting"? He was talking about those things that he relied on to have favor and right standing with God. In Philippians 3:4-6, he said:

> *...though I also might have confidence in the flesh. If anyone else thinks he may have confidence in the flesh, I more so: circumcised the eighth day, of the stock of Israel, of the tribe of Benjamin, a Hebrew of the Hebrews; concerning the law, a Pharisee; concerning zeal, persecuting the church; concerning the righteousness which is in the law, blameless.*

Paul said, "*...but now I forget those things.*" Paul would not allow prior accomplishments nor any accolades of his past to inflate his ego, or stand in the way of his relationship with God.

It also means the same for the Greek athlete who is running his race; that when you pass someone, you stop thinking about the person whom you passed and continue focusing on your goal.[25] You can pass someone up in a race and begin to focus on the person whom you passed. No, don't even think about it; just keep running. In the running of *your* race, you are going to see others pass you up and you will also pass others up. This doesn't mean you are better than them, or that they are better than you–it means that you are running your race and they are running theirs.

Some of us notice others who have not been born-again long as we have. In our minds we conclude that we've served in more capacities and been faithful longer. Yet, all of a sudden, it seems as though they are steadily advancing– being acknowledged and promoted in bless- ings. Then you begin thinking, "God, this is not fair. I have been saved longer than they have. How can this happen, God?" No. Let them run their race and you run yours. You are not supposed to be looking at them; you are supposed to be looking at Jesus.

Forgetting also includes those things that hurt us. A prime example of this is a young man named Joseph. He was hated and envied by his brothers, because God gave him dreams of a destiny in leadership. This hatred was soon acted upon, as his brothers sold him as a slave. Joseph was taken to Egypt where he was propositioned and threatened by Potiphar's wife, framed for raping her even though he was totally innocent and full of integrity, and sent to prison and forgotten. After years in prison, Joseph was called upon to interpret two dreams that troubled Pharaoh. The chief butler, who had previously forgotten about Joseph's accurate interpretation of his own dream, remembered him. When Pharaoh heard the interpretation of his dreams, and Joseph's plan for storing food during times of abundance for the times of famine, he promoted him. Joseph became second in command in the most powerful nation at that time. Pharaoh also gave Joseph a wife named Asenath and from this union they had two boys.

The names of Joseph's sons are pertinent to the topic of forgetting those circumstances and people who wronged us. The name of Joseph's firstborn was Manasseh, which means, "God has made me forget all my toil and all my father's house". The name of the second boy was Ephraim: "...for God has caused me to be fruitful in the land of my affliction" (Genesis 41:51-52). There's a powerful truth related to the order and meaning of these names, which is that we must be able to forget before we can become fruitful. Although this may be easier said then done, God has a way of making us forget by restoring and renewing our minds.

The best result of forgetting is the ability for you to then reach for a better future and move forward again. The imagery of this is of a runner who is straining with everything that is within him toward the finish line. You may feel like you don't have a future, but you do and, friend, it is bright. God has things that are laid out in front of you, both to have and to do, but you must reach for them. His promises are close enough to where you can see them, but far enough away that you must reach out to obtain them by faith.

Although the Greek runner would be handsomely rewarded for winning, it does not compare to the reward that the Christian can receive from the Lord. You will receive an imperishable crown that is eternal. The Bible speaks of the crown of righteousness (II Timothy 4-8), the crown of life (James 1:2), and the crown of glory (I Peter 5:4). At the very end of the course that He has laid out for your life, a crown awaits you. In conjunction with that crown, God has authority for you. The word "prize", in 1 Corinthians 9:24, means "rule" or "authority"[26]. So, when God gives you that crown, He gives you authority throughout eternity. Your position in eternity is determined by what you and I do here on earth in the running of our races. Consider these verses, which are very enlightening and sobering.

In 2 John 8, *"Look to yourselves, that we do not lose those things we worked for, but that we may receive a full reward."* This would

"We could be the recipient of a "partial" reward or none."

mean that we could lose out on receiving a full reward. We could be the recipient of a "partial" reward or none because we did not run in our lane; we did not do our assigned work. Notice these words in Revelation 3:11; *"Behold, I am coming quickly! Hold fast what you have, that no one may take your crown."* The possibility exists that the crown, which has been laid out before time began for you, is not worn by you, but by someone else. The person will not literally take it from you, but will get it instead of you because he/she did the work that you were supposed to do; the work that was a part of your course was done by another. I think that we need to run our races to win and get everything done here on earth that our Heavenly Father has graciously prepared for us (Ephesians 2:10).

My final point of this chapter is to practice finishing what you've started. The purpose of starting anything is to finish. It may be a very daunting thought, when considering finishing the work God has for your life here on earth, but you can do it. In his swan song, Paul said:

I have fought the good fight, I have finished the race, I have kept the faith. Finally, there is laid up for me the crown of righteousness, which the Lord, the Righteous Judge, will give to me on that day, and not to me only, but also to all who have loved His appearing (II Timothy 4:7-8).

European myth and legend has it that a swan is mute for its entire life until moments before death; at such time, it sings a beautiful song[27]. Thus, it is a metaphorical phrase for a final gesture, effort or performance, given before death or retirement. The aged apostle knew that his course was finished and he was therefore, ready to be martyred for the faith he so diligently contended for. Finishing our races is a prerequisite to receiving our heavenly rewards, but how did Paul arrive at this place of finishing?

He probably did not foresee his end at the beginning (only God does that), but he knew there was an end; there is a principle we can learn from his life and apply to our lives. I learned what I'm about to share with you from my pastor, Bayless Conley, during a Sunday service.

In Acts 11:27-30, it says:

And in these days prophets came from Jerusalem to Antioch. Then one of them, named Agabus, stood up and showed by the Spirit that there was going to be a great famine throughout all the world, which also happened in the days of Claudius Caesar. Then the disciples, each according to his ability, determined to send relief to the brethren dwelling in Judea. This they also did, and sent it to

*the elders by the hands of Barnabas and
Saul [Paul].*

Barnabas and Saul had been chosen to take
relief to the church at Jerusalem, due to the
prophetic word given by Agabus the prophet.
For anyone sensing a call of God in his/her life,
taking food to another church may not be the
thing that you would sign up for. The truth is
there are no insignificant tasks when it comes
to helping people–especially not to God.

Notice in Acts 12:25: *"And Barnabas and
Saul returned from Jerusalem, when they had
fulfilled their ministry, and took with them
John, whose surname was Mark."* This verse
defines what Barnabas and Paul did as "ministry". Our thinking of ministry may only be
relegated to preaching, teaching, singing and
praying for the sick. Yet, this verse broadens

our perspectives of ministry and further teaches us the importance of fulfilling our ministries.

Why is finishing so important? It opens up the door for the next phase of your race that God has laid out before you. I believe that as we are faithful in the small things, then God entrusts us with more. If we are not faithful to complete what God has given us, more cannot be given. Read what happened to Barnabas and Saul in Acts 13: 1-4:

"Now in the church that was at Antioch there were certain prophets and teachers; Barnabas, Simeon who was called Niger, Lucius of Cyrene, Manaen who had been brought up with Herod the tetrarch, and Saul."

Barnabas and Saul were sent out into apostolic ministry, or what we commonly call missionaries. The Holy Spirit did not just speak out of the air, but through one or two of the prophets and teachers listed in verse one. This release into the next phase of their races would not have occurred unless they had fin- ished their ministry to bring food to

"...we cannot move in to what the Lord has next if we've not completed what's in front of us today."

Jerusalem. Our races are composed of different phases and seasons, and we cannot move in to what the Lord has next if we have not completed what is in front of us today.

Win–Thoughts on Training to Win

1. Consider a circumstance in your life today. Which promise of God can you apply by obeying the truth?

2. Stir yourself to live for and serve God wholeheartedly, no matter your position or audience, because you are serving Jesus.

3. Remember temperance, or abstinence, applies to every indulgence that would render the body weak. Where can you apply temperance today?

4. Exercise focus and gratitude as God progresses and promotes you, without giving attention to whom you may have advanced passed.

5. *Contemplate on the fact that you can receive a full reward for finishing the work God has called you to do. This will determine your authority throughout eternity.*

6. *Be faithful in the small things, because this is the catalyst of God's movement forward in your life*

CHAPTER 7

GOD RUNS TO YOU

GOD RUNS TO YOU

*O*ne day I came across this inspiring poem written by Dr. D.H Groberg called–you guessed it–"The Race". It's about boys who were running a competitive race, with a crowd eagerly watching in the stands. The poem focuses on one boy who wanted to win and make his dad proud.

As he ran, the unthinkable happened and the boy fell, not once or twice, but three times. The crowd had laughed at him before, but in the midst of the nameless, faceless crowd, he found his father and the look that beamed from his father's eyes said, "Get up and win

the race!" Here's what occurred after the third
and final fall.

Defeat! He lay there silently
—A tear dropped from his eye—
"There's no sense running anymore;
Three strikes: I'm out! Why try!"

The will to rise had disappeared;
All hope had fled away;
So far behind, so error prone;
A loser all the way.

"I've lost, so what's the use," he thought
"I'll live with my disgrace."
But then he thought about his dad
Who soon he'd have to face.

"Get up," an echo sounded low.
"Get up and take your place;
You were not meant for failure here.
Get up and win the race."

"With borrowed will get up," it said,
"You haven't lost at all.
For winning is no more than this:
To rise each time you fall."

So up he rose to run once more,
And with a new commit
He resolved that win or lose
At least he wouldn't quit.

So far behind the others now,
—The most he'd ever been—
Still he gave it all he had
And ran as though to win.

Three times he'd fallen, stumbling;
Three times he rose again;
Too far behind to hope to win
He still ran to the end.

They cheered the winning runner
As he crossed the line first place.

Head high, and proud, and happy;
No falling, no disgrace.

But when the fallen youngster
Crossed the line last place,
The crowd gave him the greater cheer,
For finishing the race.

And even though he came in last
With head bowed low, unproud,
You would have thought he'd won the race
To listen to the crowd.

And to his dad he sadly said,
"I didn't do too well."
"To me, you won," his father said.
You rose each time you fell."

And now when things seem dark and hard
And difficult to face,
The memory of that little boy
Helps me in my race.

For all of life is like that race,

With ups and downs and all.

And all you have to do to win,

Is rise each time you fall.

"Quit! Give up! You're beaten!"

They still shout in my face.

But another voice within me says:

"GET UP AND WIN THE RACE!"[28]

I want you to know today that you're not alone—God is with you. When Moses, the iconic legendary leader who led over two million of God's people out of Egyptian slavery into freedom died, it was a sad, sad day in Israel. Now Joshua, Moses's assistant, had to take the baton of leadership to lead the people into their inheritance. What would God say to him? What would Israel's new leader need to hear?

"No man shall be able to stand before you all the days of your life. As I was with Moses, so I will be with you. I will not leave you nor forsake you," *(Joshua 1:5).*

I'm certain this affirmation bolstered Joshua's heart with courage and confidence for him to rise up and lead. Knowing God was with him gave Joshua what he needed most – inward assurance.

Before Jesus was about to be crucified, He spoke often to His disciples about the Person and ministry of the Holy Spirit. Jesus said, in John 14:16, *"And I will pray the Father, and He will give you another Helper, that He may abide with you forever."*

The word "another" is the Greek word "allos", which means another of the same kind.[29] The Holy Spirit would be to the disciples what Jesus was to them while He was physically alive with them. Before Christ ascended, He assured the disciples that He would be with them always, even to the end of the age (Matthew 28:20).

So, the disciples would be running their races to preach the gospel to the world, and make disciples of the nations, but they would not be alone—God would run with them. Knowing God is with you will strengthen you and give you the courage to do what He was set before

"If you should fall along your course, that does not mean your race is over, it means that you have to get back up, dust yourself and keep going."

you. If you should fall along your course, that does not mean your race is over; it means that you have to get back up, dust yourself and keep going.

"For a righteous man may fall seven times and rise again..." (Proverbs 24:16)

In the 1992 Olympic games in Barcelona, Spain, a very inspirational and unforgettable moment occurred. Derek Anthony Redmond, a British athlete, was favored to win the 400-meter race. In the semi-final race, it appeared that Derek would be victorious, but with about 175 meters to go, he tore his hamstring. This is a very painful injury. He fell to the ground and began to cry, not just because of the pain, but because his hopes of advancing to the finals and winning the medal were gone. Derek Redmond could've dropped out of the race, but he got up and began to hobble on one leg. Later he said, "I was doing it for me. Whether people thought I was an idiot or a hero, I wanted to finish the race..." Once the crowd realized he was continuing to run, they began to cheer.

Derek's father, Jim Redmond, ran out of the stands, jumped over the railing, avoided a security guard and ran to his son to help him. Jim said, "I'm

"Jim said, "I'm here son. We'll finish together."

here, son. We'll finish together." He put his arm around his father's shoulder and wept. They finished together.[30]

Perhaps you've been running your race, but feel like something has been torn in your life. Maybe you feel like your heart has been torn because of what has been going on with your children, your marriage or your work. You may feel torn financially because you've lost possessions, a home or a job.

The number one message that surfaces from the aforementioned story is that in spite of the pain, Derek Redmond found enough courage to try and still run; he didn't quit. The second message is that his father saw his son trying, hurting and disappointed, but still trying to run. Jim's love for his son could not keep him in the stands.

If an earthly father would do this for his son, how much more would your Heavenly Father do this for you? (Luke 11:11) Your Heavenly Father wants you to know today that He is coming to you to put His arms around you. He will hold on to you and you hold on to Him, and you'll finish your race together.

This scene is also portrayed in the life of a young man attempting to run in the wrong lane. This young man ran away from everything that was good and right in his life, because he was only thinking about himself and his immediate short-lived pleasure. He prematurely obtained his inheritance and wasted it all on riotous living. When the money ran out, so did his fair-weathered friends, and he found himself in a foreign place, alone, hungry and empty. He was so desperate that he took on an extremely shameful occupation, according to his cultural and religious heritage. He was so famished that he was about to eat the food of the animals that he was taking care of; he had hit rock bottom.

As bad as this sounds, it was good, because he finally woke up and came to himself. You see, his decision to disconnect from his father and follow his desires instead of his father's plan (his race) had caused him to lose himself — his identity and his purpose in life. It dawned on him what he must do. "I'm going back to my father. I'll say to him, 'Father, I've sinned against God, I've sinned before you; I don't deserve to be called your son. Take me on as a hired hand.'" He got right up and went home to his father. When he was still a long way off, his father saw him. His heart pounding,

"When he was still along way off, his father saw him. His heart pounding, HE RAN OUT, embraced him, and kissed him."

HE RAN OUT, embraced his son and kissed him. The son started his speech:

> *"Father, I've sinned against God, I've sinned before you; I don't deserve to be called your son ever again." But the father wasn't listening. He was calling to the servants, "Quick, bring a clean set of clothes and dress him. Put the family ring on his finger and sandals on his feet. Then get a grain-fed heifer and roast it. We're going to feast! We're going to have a wonderful time! My son is here – given up for dead, and now alive! Given up for lost and now found! They began to have a wonderful time,"* (Luke 15: 18-24, The Message).[31]

My friend, I don't believe it is an accident you are reading this book. Maybe your life is reflective of the young man in this story, known as the prodigal son. Perhaps there was a time in your life when you were passionate about living for God, involved in the life of your local church–running your race. Yet due to a loss of focus, disappointment, bad choices or company, you find yourself away from the sweet fellowship of your Heavenly Father. Now is your moment to repent from going your own way, turn around and come back to Him. When you do this, I can tell you what will happen. Your Father will RUN TO YOU. He will neither judge nor condemn, but instead will embrace, love, restore, and rejoice in your return. His Presence will cleanse and wash over your soul, and once you've been strengthened, He will put you back in the race. Then run with a renewed focus – run to win.

God Runs To You–Thoughts on Training to Win

1. *Remind yourself that the Holy Spirit is with you today, just as Jesus was with His disciples.*

2. *Know that God will strengthen you if you've fallen, so you can rise up and run your race.*

3. *Meditate on the truth that God runs to help you and will not judge, but restore you.*

CHAPTER 8

ENTERING THE RACE

ENTERING THE RACE

$\mathcal{E}$very race or competition is won by an individual or team that has entered the event. I've never witnessed someone winning a game or an event that they had not rightfully entered into.

In the previous chapters, there was much discussion on winning our Christian races, but you cannot win your race if you have not entered the race. It's normal to have some prerequisites in a competitive event. It's also understandable that the best in any given area of competition would be the ones battling for victory. Those who do not qualify may pay and enjoy watching the event, but will never be able to compete in the activity or sport of their desire.

In the Greek games, there were certain criteria that had to be met in order to participate. A person had to be of Greek origin, a male and a free man. It should be noted that the participants came from families that were well-off. Women, slaves and foreigners were not allowed to compete. Imagine having a desire and the skill to compete, but because you were not in a select group, you were not allowed to participate. Even if one of these were athletically qualified and worked as hard as the participants, they still could not compete.

I think when it comes to having a relationship with God, many are working hard at trying to qualify. These individuals believe their good deeds, religious rituals, philanthropic involvement or their "good outweighing their bad" causes them to win in their relationship with God. Ephesians 2:8-9 states, *"For by grace you have been saved through faith, and not that of yourselves, it is the gift of God, not of works, lest anyone should boast."*

These verses tell us that you don't have to work or qualify in order to have a relationship with God. Christianity is not for the rich and famous, nor for the impoverished and unpopular. Christianity is founded and centered on the Person of Jesus Christ, who loves us and came to save us. It is for *"...whoever believes on Him"* and for *"...whoever calls on the name of the Lord shall be saved,"* (Romans 10:13).

No matter who you are, where you are, or what you've done, the invitation to enter this race is extended to you. Baron Batch, a former collegiate football player from Texas Tech University, said, "If you are a thousand steps away from God...God will take 999 steps just so you will take that one".[32] Here is the one key step to take to God and to enter your race. Pray this prayer:

> Dear God,
>
> I come just as I am to confess my deep need of You. I believe that You love me and sent Jesus to die in my place on the cross. I believe that because of His shed blood, all of my sins are forgiven. I believe that You raised Jesus up from the grave, and today I confess Him as the Lord of my life. Thank You for making me a new creation in Christ. Amen.

ACKNOWLEDGMENTS

I would like to thank the following persons for their contribution to the completion of this project: my wife Angel, for her support, prayers, encouragement and patience; Vera Mulkey, my mother, for her love, example and support throughout my life; Andrea Bolder, Joel Holm and John Howard, my endorsers, for taking time to read and provide a thoughtful response; Pastor Bayless Conley, my pastor and friend whose calling to communicate truth has inspired and broadened my spiritual life; Lisa Lopez, my project coordinator, whose diligence and administrative skills helped bring this to completion; Pastor Dan Kotoff, for his initial editorial assistance; Jackie Priestley, editor, for her ability and skill to clarify thought; best selling author, Deborah Pegues, bringing needed direction with her insight, counsel, and provision of resources; Mike Edwards Photography, for their spirit of excellence; Freddie and Tyren Alvidrez for bringing the chapter titles into picture form; to my Cottonwood Church family for your love, prayers, kindness and encouragement; and to my Lord and Savior Jesus, who gave me life.

ENDNOTES

[1] Knox, Ronald, Knox Bible; Baronius Press; October 15, 2012

[2] Williams, B., Charles; The New Testament in the Language of the People Holman Bible Publishers Nashville, TN; 1937 (reprinted 1986).

[3] Several: The Olympic Games in Antiquity www.olympic.org/.../the_olympic_games/en_report_658.pdf

[4] Several: The Olympic Games in Antiquity www.olympic.org/.../the_olympic_games/en_report_658.pdf

[5] Several: The Olympic Games in Antiquity www.olympic.org/.../the_olympic_games/ en_report_658.pdf

[6] Chinander, Allie Fantasy Casting: "Gold Medal Summer: The Michael Phelps Story" ; www.sikids.com; August 6, 2013.

[7] Chinander, Allie; Fantasy Casting: "Gold Medal Summer: The Michael Phelps Story"; www.sikids.com August 6, 2013.

[8] Assisi, St. Francis of The Little Flowers of St. Francis of Assisi; www.goodreads.com Published March 24, 1998 by Vintage (first published 1390).

[9] Siewert, Francis E; The Amplified Bible; Zondervan; Grand Rapids, 1965 (revised 1987).

[10] Mass Moments: Rosie Ruiz Steals Boston Marathon; Massachusetts Foundation for the Humanities; April 21, 2006.

[11] Burt, Bill; Rosie's Run; The Eagle-Tribune; April 16, 2000.

Moore, Kenny, Mastery and Mystery; Sports Illustrated; April 28, 1986.

[12] Several: The Olympic Games in Antiquity; www.olympic.org/.../the_olympic_games/ en_report_658.pdf

[13] Strong, James S.T.D., LL.D; Strong's Exhaustive Concordance of the Bible; Riverside Book and Bible House; Iowa Falls, Iowa 50126.

[14] Several: The Olympic Games in Antiquity; www.olympic.org/.../the_olympic_games/ en_report_658.pdf

[15] Strong, James S.T.D., LL.D Strong's Exhaustive Concordance of the Bible Riverside Book and Bible House; Iowa Falls, Iowa 50126.

[16] Barnes, Albert; Barnes Notes; Database Copyright © 1997, 2003, 2005, 2006; Biblesoft, Inc.

[17] Strong, James S.T.D., LL.D; Strong's Exhaustive Concordance of the Bible; Riverside Book and Bible House; Iowa Falls, Iowa 50126.

[18] Weymouth, Richard, Francis; The New Testament in Modern Speech; Lutterworth Press; November 26, 1987.

[19] Taylor, Kenneth; The Living Bible Tyndale House 1971.

[20] Strong, James S.T.D., LL.D; Strong's Exhaustive Concordance of the Bible; Riverside Book and Bible House Iowa Falls, Iowa 50126.

[21] Strong, James S.T.D., LL.D Strong's Exhaustive Concordance of the Bible Riverside Book and Bible House; Iowa Falls, Iowa 50126.

[22] Hewett, James; Illustrations Unlimited; Tyndale House Publishers; July 15, 1988.

[23] Several: The Olympic Games in Antiquity; www.olympic.org/.../the_olympic_games/en_report_658.pdf

[24] Several: The Olympic Games in Antiquity www.olympic.org/.../the_olympic_games/en_report_658.pdf

[25] Barnes, Albert; Barnes' Notes; Database Copyright © 1997, 2003, 2005, 2006; Biblesoft Inc.

[26] Strong, James S.T.D., LL.D; Strong's Exhaustive Concordance of the Bible; Riverside Book and Bible House; Iowa Falls, Iowa 50126.

[27] Tenneson, Alfred, Lord "The Dying Swan" Macmillan and Co.; London 1830.

[28] Used by permission of the author, Dr. D. H. (Dee) Groberg.

[29] Strong, James S.T.D., LL.D; Strong's Exhaustive Concordance of the Bible; Riverside Book and Bible House; Iowa Falls, Iowa 50126.

[30] Weinberg, Rick: Derek and dad finish Olympic 400 together; http://espn.go.com/olympics/story/_/id/7445920/2012-london-games-derek-redmond-father-carry-olym-pic-torch

Flip Bondy; Barcelona: Track and Field; British Runner is a Hero Even Without a Medal www.nytimes.com; August 5, 1992.

Lee, Honeyball; 'I hated the world, then I felt a hand on my shoulder' www.theguardian.com; January 6, 2007.

[31] Peterson, Eugene, H.; The Message – The Bible in Contemporary Language; Nav Press Publishing Group; Colorado Springs, Colorado; 2002.

[32] Riley, Jennifer; Football Star: God Will Take 999 Steps for You to Take One; www.christianpost.com/news/football; November 15, 2001.